Best Joke Book for Kids

Peter MacDonald

ISBN-13: 978-1492868064
ISBN-10: 149286806X:

Contents

Best Jokes for Kids

As kids grow older they find certain jokes less and less funny. This means you have to come up with age appropriate jokes to keep them entertained. Jokes are more than just for laughs. They also stimulate thought and educate. That does not mean you go stiff on the kids, far from it. You want jokes that are funny, corny and have some substance. Usually the really good jokes will give even you the tickles.

Kids can be pretty critical and they are not afraid to let you know *"You're just not funny!"* Here 's a bit of help for you – 200+ jokes for kids between ages 10 and 14. Here goes.

30 Simple Jokes for Whetting the Appetite

1. **Q:** Knock, knock. Who's there?

A: Lettuce

Q: Lettuce who?

A: Lettuce in, it's freezing out here..

2. **Q:** What do elves learn in school?

A: The elf-abet

3. **Q:** Why was 6 afraid of 7?

A: Because: 7 8 9

4. **Q.** how do you make seven an even number?

A. Take out the **s**!

5. **Q:** Which dog can jump higher than a building?

A: Anydog – Buildings can't jump!

6. **Q:** Why do bananas have to put on sunscreen before they go to the beach?

A: Because they might peel!

7. **Q.** How do you make a tissue dance?

A. You put a little boogie in it.

8. **Q:** Which flower talks the most?

A: Tulips, of course, 'cause they have *two* lips!

9. Q: Where do pencils go for vacation?

A: Pencil-vania

10. Q: What did the mushroom say to the fungus?

A: You're a fun guy [fungi].

11. Q: Why did the girl smear peanut butter on the road?

A: To go with the traffic jam!

11. Q: What do you call cheese that's not yours?

A: Nacho cheese!

12. Q: Why are ghosts bad liars?

A: Because you can see right through them.

13. **Q:** Why did the boy bring a ladder to school?

A: He wanted to go to high school.

14. **Q:** How do you catch a unique animal?

A: You neak up on it.

Q: How do you catch a tame one?

A: Tame way.

15. **Q:** Why is the math book always mad?

A: Because it has so many problems.

16. **Q.** What animal would you not want to pay cards with?

A. Cheetah

17. **Q:** What was the broom late for school?

A: Because it over swept.

18. **Q:** What music do balloons hate?

A: Pop music.

19. **Q:** Why did the baseball player take his bat to the library?

A: Because his teacher told him to hit the books.

20. **Q:** What did the judge say when the skunk walked in the court room?
A: Odor in the court!

21. **Q:** Why are fish so smart?

A: Because they live in schools.

22. **Q:** What happened when the lion ate the comedian?

A: He felt funny!

23. **Q:** What animal has more lives than a cat?

A: Frogs, they croak every night!

24. **Q:** What do you get when you cross a snake and a pie?

A: A pie-thon!

25. **Q:** Why is a fish easy to weigh?

A: Because it has its own scales!

26. **Q:** Why aren't elephants allowed on beaches?

A: They can't keep their trunks up!

27. **Q:** How did the barber win the race?

A: He knew a shortcut!

28. **Q:** Why was the man running around his bed?

A: He wanted to catch up on his sleep.

29. **Q:** Why is 6 afraid of 7?

A: Because 7 8 9!

.

30. **Q:** What is a butterfly's favorite subject at school?
A: Mothematics.

Jokes by Categories

20 Mixed Animal Jokes

Have you heard the one about a cat

Animal jokes are some of the funniest jokes around. Here are a few jokes about different animals. Specific groups will have a fun fact that be shared before going into the jokes.

1. **Q:** What do you call a sleeping bull?

A: A bull-dozer.

2. **Q:** What to polar bears eat for lunch?

A: Ice berg-ers!

3. **Q:** What do you get from a pampered cow?

A: Spoiled milk.

4. **Q:** What do you call a bear with no teeth?

A: A gummy bear!

5. **Q:** Why are teddy bears never hungry?

A: They are always stuffed!

6. **Q:** What bird is always sad?

A: The blue jay!

7. **Q.** What did the porcupine say to the cactus?

A. "Is that you mommy?

8. **Q.** Why do sea-gulls fly over the sea?

A. Because if they flew over the bay they would be bagels!

9. **Q:** Why did the snake cross the road?

A: To get to the other sssssside!

10. Knock Knock!

Who's there?

Kook!

Kook who?

Don't call me cuckoo!

11. **Q.** What did the fish say when he swam into the wall?

A. Dam!

12. **Q:** Why are frogs so happy?

A: Because they eat what bugs them!

13. **Q:** What do you get when you cross a walrus with a bee?

A: A wallaby!

14. **Q:** What's the most musical part of a chicken?

A: The drumstick!

15. **Q:** Why didn't the dinosaur cross the road?

A: There were no roads back then!

16. **Q:** A rooster laid an egg on a barn roof. Which way would it roll?

A: Roosters don't lay eggs, hens do!

17. **Q:** Why don't oysters share their pearls?

A: Because they're shellfish!

18. **Q:** What do you call a girl with a frog in her hair?

A: Lily!

19. **Q:** What types of horses only go out at night?

A: Nightmares!

20. **Q:** Someone said you sounded like an owl.

A: Who?

10 Chicken Jokes

Fun fact: The sounds they make are actually their language (chicken language). Each alarm cry is different, and made to signify the type of predator that is threatening them.

1. **Q:** How do chickens bake a cake?

A: From scratch!

2. **Q:** Where do tough chickens come from?

A: Hard-boiled eggs!

3. **Q:** What do you get if you cross a cocker spaniel, a poodle and a rooster?

A: Cockerpoodledoo!

4. **Q:** What do you get if you cross a chicken with a cow?

A: Roost beef!

5. **Q:** Chickens rise when the rooster crows, but when do ducks get up?

A: At the quack of dawn!

6. **Q:** Why do hens lay eggs?

A: If they dropped them, they'd break!

7. **Q:** What does an evil hen lay?

A: Deviled eggs!

8. **Q:** Why did the hen cross the road?

A: To prove she wasn't a chicken!

9. **Q.** What day do chickens hate most?

A. Fry-days!

10. **Q.** Which side of a chicken has more feathers?

A. The outside.

10 Fish Jokes

Fun fact: As it relates to their to their body size, fish have small brains compared to that of most other animals.

1. **Q:** Where do fish sleep?

A: On a seabed!

2. **Q:** What do you get when you cross a shark and a snowman?

A: Frostbite!

3. **Q:** What's the most musical part of a fish?

A: The scales!

4. **Q:** What's the difference between a piano and a fish?

A: You can tune a piano, but you can't tuna fish.

5. **Q:** How do oysters call their friends?

A: On shell phones!

6. **Q:** What is the strongest creature in the sea?

A: A mussel!

7. **Q:** Where do fish keep their money?

A: In a river-bank!

8. **Q:** What do fish and maps have in common?

A: They both have scales!

9. **Q:** What lives in the ocean, is grouchy and hates neighbors?

A: A hermit crab!

10. **Q:** What do you call a fish without an eye?
A: fsh!

10 Cat Jokes

Fun fact: A cat whips its tail when it's in a bad mood. That means it's best for you to keep your distance!

1. **Q:** What kind of cats like to go bowling?

A: Alley cats!

2. **Q:** What is a cat's favorite color?

A: Purr-ple!

3. **Q:** What game did the cat like to play with the mouse?

A: Catch!

4. **Q:** Who was the first cat to fly in an airplane?

A: Kitty-hawk

5. **Q:** Why are cats good at video games?

A: Because they have nine lives!

.6. **Q:** What animal is bad to play games with?

A: A cheetah!

7. **Q:** What did the cat have for breakfast?

A: Mice Crispies!

8. **Q:** Why can't a leopard hide?

A: Because it's always spotted!

9. **Q:** What state has a lot of cats and dogs?

A: Petsylvania

10. **Q:** Have you ever seen a catfish?

A: No. I don't think he could he hold the rod and reel?

10 Dog Jokes

Fun fact: The shape of a dog's face gives a hint about how long it will live. Those with sharp, pointed faces (wolf-like) usually live longer than those with flat faces.

1. **Q:** What do you call a dog that is left handed?

A: A south paw!

2. **Q:** Why did the snowman call his dog "Frost"?

A: Because Frost-bites!

3. **Q:** When is a dog not a dog?

A: When it is pure bred/bread!

4. **Q:** Why did the poor dog chase its own tail?

A: It was trying to make ends meet.

5. **Q:** What do you get when you cross a sheep dog with a rose?

A: A collie-flower.

6. **Q:** Why didn't the dog speak to its foot?

A: Because it is not polite to speak back to your paw.

7. **Q:** What did the dog say when he sat on the sandpaper?

A: Ruff!

8. **Q:** What did one flee say to the other?

A: Should we walk or take a dog?

9. **Q:** What's worse than raining cats and dogs?

A: Hailing Taxis!

10. **Q:** How do you call a dog with no legs?

A: It doesn't matter how you call him. He still won't come!

10 Bear Jokes

Fun Fact: Some Native Americans call bears "the beast that walks like a man," because they can walk short distances on their hind legs.

1. **Q:** What is a bear's favorite drink?

A: Koka-Koala!

2. **Q:** What do you call bears with no ears?

A: B!

3. **Q:** Why do bears have fur coats?

A: Because they look silly wearing jackets!.

4. **Q:** How do you start a teddy bear race?

A: Teddy, Set, Go!

5. **Q:** How do Teddy bears send their letters?

A: By bear mail!

6. **Q:** What color socks do bears wear?

A: They don't wear socks, they have bear feet!

7. **Q:** What do teddy bears do when it rains?

A: They get wet!

8. **Q:** What do you get if you cross a grizzly bear with a harp?

A: A bear faced lyre!

9. **Q:** How do teddies keep their houses cool in the summer?

A: They use bear conditioning!

10. **Q:** What do bears buy when they go to the shops?

A: They buy the bear necessities!

10 Elephant Jokes

Fun fact: Of all the mammals in the world only one cannot jump, and that is the elephant.

1. Q. Why doesn't the elephant use a computer?

A. Because it is afraid of the mouse!

2. **Q:** What game do you NOT want to play with an elephant?

A: Squash!

3. **Q:** How do you stop an elephant from charging?

A: Take away her credit card!

4. **Q.** Why do elephants need trunks?

A. Because they don't have glove compartments!

.

5. Q. What's big and grey with red spots?

A. An elephant with the measles!

.

6. **Q:** Why are elephants so wrinkled?

A: They take too long to iron!

7. **Q:** How do elephants talk to each other long distance?

A: On the elephone! They make trunk calls.

8. **Q:** Why are elephants so poor?

A: Because they work for peanuts!

9. **Q:** What do elephants do in the evenings?

A: Watch elevision!

10. **Q:** What does a doctor give an elephant who's going to be sick?

A: Plenty of room!.

10 Cow Jokes

Fun fact: A female cattle that has given birth is called a cow while one that has not given birth is called a heifer.

1. **Q:** What do you call a cow with no legs ?

A: Ground Beef!

2. **Q:** Why does a milking stool have only three legs?

A: Because it the cow has the udder!

3. **Q:** Why do cows wear bells?

A: Their horns don't work.

4. **Q:** What do cows get when they get sick?

A: Hay fever!

5. **Q:** Where do cows go on a Friday night?

A: To the moo-vies!

6. **Q:** What happened to the lost cattle?

A: Nobody's herd!

7. **Q:** What do you get when you cross a cow and a goat?

A: A coat!

8. **Q:** What did the cow look wearing a horse costume?

A: Udderly ridiculous!!!

9. **Q:** What did the farmer call the cow that had no milk?

A: An udder failure!

10. Knock Knock!

Who's there?

Cowsgo

Cowsgo who? No they don't, cows-go moo.

10 Knock Knock Jokes

1. Knock Knock!

Who's there?

Canoe!

Canoe who?

Canoe come over and play.

2. Knock Knock!

Who's there?

Figs.

Figs who?

Figs the doorbell, it's broken!

3. Knock Knock!

Who's there?

Abby!

Abby who?

Abby birthday to you.

4. Knock Knock!

Who's there?

Justin!

Justin who?

Justin time for lunch.

5. Knock Knock!

Who's there?

Interrupting cow.

Interrupt...

Moo! (Say moo before the asker can complete the question "Interrupt cow who?")

6. Knock Knock!

Who's there?

Tank !

Tank who?

Your welcome.

.

7. Knock knock!

Who's there?

Little old lady?

Little old lady who?

Wow! I didn't know you could yodel!

8. Knock knock!

Who's there?

Owls say!

Owls say who?

Yep

9. Knock knock!

Who's there?

Dewey.

Dewey who?

Dewey have to keep telling silly jokes.

10. Knock Knock!

Who's there?

Boo!

Boo who?

Don't cry, Easter Bunny comes back next year!

10 Math Jokes

1. **Q:** Why didn't the quarter roll down the hill with the nickel?

A: Because it had more cents.

2. **Q:** What do you get when you divide the circumference of a Jack-o-lantern by its diameter?

A: Pumpkin Pi!

3. **Q:** What snakes are good at doing sums?

A: Adders!

4. **Q:** Teacher: Why are you doing your multiplication on the floor?

A: Student: You told me not to use tables.

5. **Q:** What is a math teacher's favorite sum?

A: Summer!

6. **Q:** What kind of meals do math teachers eat?

A: Square meals!

7. **Q:** What did zero say to the number eight?

A: Nice belt.

8. **Q:** Why did the two 4's skip lunch?

A: They already 8!

9. **Q:** What is a mathematician's favorite dessert?

A: Pi!

10. **Q:** If you had 8 apples in one hand and 5 apples in the other, what would you have?

A: Really big hands!

15 Food Jokes

1. **Q:** Why was the cucumber mad?

A: Because it was in a pickle!

2. **Q:** What do you call cheese that's not yours?

A: Nacho cheese!

.

3. **Q:** What's wrong with a restaurant on the moon?

A: It has no atmosphere!

4. **Q:** What did the nut say when it sneezed?

A: Cashew!

5. **Q:** What does a mixed up hen lay?

A: Scrambled eggs!

6. **Q:** What bird is with you every time you eat?

A: A swallow!

7. **Q:** Why did the banana have to leave in a hurry?

A: Because it had to split!

8. **Q:** What do you get when you cross a frog and a popsicle?

A: A hopsicle!

9. **Q:** What kind of plates do they use in space?

A: Flying saucers!

10. **Q:** What do ghosts like for dessert?

A: I scream!

11. **Q:** What day do potatoes hate the most?

A: Fry-day!

12. **Q:** What do sea monsters eat for lunch?

A: Fish and ships!

13. **Q:** Why was the cookie sad?

A: Because her mom was a-wafer so long!

.

14. **Q:** What do snowmen like to eat for breakfast?

A: Frosted Flakes!

15. **Q:** Why was the strawberry sad?

A: Because her mom was in a jam!

15 Doctor and Dentists Jokes

1. **Q:** Why did the house go to the doctor?

A: Because it had a window pain!

2. **Q:** How does a frog feel when she has a broken leg?

A: Unhoppy!

3. **Q:** Where do ghosts go when they're sick?

A: To the witch doctor!

4. **Q:** Why did the pillow go to the doctor?

A: He was feeling all stuffed up!

5. **Q:** Why didn't the girl tell the doctor that she ate some glue?

A: Her lips were sealed!

6. **Q:** What did on tonsil say to the other tonsil?

.A: Get dressed up, the doctor is taking us out

7. **Q:** When does a doctor get mad?

A: When he runs out of patients!

8. **Q:** What do you give a sick bird?

A: Tweet-ment!

9. **Q:** Did you hear the one about the germ?

A: Never mind, I don't want to spread it around

10. **Patient:** I feel like everyone is ignoring me.

Doctor: Next!

11. **Patient:** Doctor, I think I need glasses!

Waiter: You certainly do, this is a restaurant!

12. **Patient:** Doctor, sometimes I feel like I'm invisible.

Doctor: Who said that?

13. **Patient:** I think I'm a pair of curtains!

Doctor: Pull yourself together!

14. **Patient:** Doctor, I keep hearing a ringing sound.

Doctor: Then answer the phone!

15. **Patient:** I swallowed a lot of food coloring.

Doctor: You'll be okay.

Patient: But I feel like I've dyed a little inside!

20 Monster Jokes

1. **Q:** Why are graveyards noisy?

A: Because of all the coffin!

2. **Q:** What position does a ghost play in soccer?

A: Ghoulie!

3. **Q:** What do witches put on their bagels?

A: Scream cheese!

4. **Q:** Where does Dracula keep his money?

A: In a blood bank!

5. **Q:** What monster plays tricks on Halloween?

A: Prank-enstein!

6. **Q:** How does a witch tell time?

A: With a witch watch!

7. **Q:** What did the skeleton order for dinner?

A: Spare ribs!

8. **Q:** Who won the skeleton beauty contest?

A: No body!

9. **Q:** Where do baby ghosts go during the day?

A: Dayscare!

10. **Q:** What do witches put on their hair?

A: Scare spray!

.

11. **Q:** What breed of dog does Dracula have?

A: A bloodhound!

12. **Q:** What's a monster's favorite play?

A: Romeo and Ghouliet!

13. **Q:** Why did the vampire get thrown out of the haunted house?

A: Because he was a pain in the neck!

14. **Q:** Which circus performers can see in the dark?

A: The acro-bats!

15. **Q:** What do ghosts use to clean their hair?

A: Sham-boo!

16. **Q:** What's a ghosts favorite desert?

A: BOO- berry pie!

17. **Q:** Where do ghosts collect their letters?

A: At the GHOST office

18. **Q:** What do baby ghosts wear on their feet?

A: BOO-tees

.

19. **Q:** Where do ghosts buy their food?

A: At the ghost-ery store.

20. **Q:** What did the boy ghost say to the girl ghost?

A: You look boo-tiful tonight.

10 Color Jokes

1. **Q :** What's orange and sounds like a parrot?

A: A carrot!

2. **Q:** What is a cheerleader's favorite color?

A: Yeller!

3. **Q:** What color is a ghost?

A: Boo!

4. **Q:** What's blue and smells like red paint?

A: Blue paint.

.

5. **Q:** What color is an echo?

A: YELL-ooohhhhhhhhhhhhhhhhh!

6. **Q:** What color is a marriage?

A: Wed

7. **Q:** What color is a baby ghost?

A: Baby boo Yellow!

8. **Q:** What color is a police investigation?

A: Copper!

9. **Q:** What do you do when you find a blue elephant?

A: Cheer her up!

10. **Q:** What happens when you throw a white hat into the Black Sea?

A: It gets wet!

10 Body Jokes

1. **Q:** How do you make a skeleton laugh?

A: Tickle her funny bone!

2. **Q:** What smells the best at dinner?

A: Your nose!

3. **Q:** What did the left eye say to the right eye?

A: Something between us smells!

4. **Q:** What's the most musical bone?

A: The trom-bone!

5. **Q:** What was served to the cannibal who was late to dinner?

A: They gave her the cold shoulder!

6. **Q:** What kind of hair do oceans have?

A: Wavy!

7. **Q:** What kind of flower grows on your face?

A: Tulips!

8. **Q:** Why didn't the skeleton cross the road?

A: It didn't have the guts!

.

9. **Q:** What has one eye but cannot see?

A: A needle!

10. **Q:** Did you pick your nose?

A: No, I was born with it!

10 Clothes Jokes

1. **Q:** What does a cloud wear under her raincoat?

A: Thunderwear!

2. **Q:** What are a ghost's favorite pants?

A: Boo jeans!

3. **Q:** What's the biggest problem with snow boots?

A: They melt!

4. **Q:** What kind of ties do pigs wear?

A: Pigs-ties!

5. **Q:** Where do frogs leave their hats and coats?

A: In the croakroom!

6. **Q:** What did the shoes say to the hat?

A: You go on a-head, I'll follow you on foot!

7. **Q:** What is the difference between a nicely-dressed man on a tricycle and a poorly dressed man on a bicycle?

A: A tire!

8. **Q:** What do penguins wear on their heads?

A: Ice caps!

9. **Q:** What goes up when the rain comes down?

A: An umbrella!

10. **Q:** What did the baseball glove say to the baseball?

A: Catch you later!

30 More Random Jokes

1. **Q:** What did the judge say when the skunk walked in the court room?

A: Odor in the court!

2. **Q:** Where do sheep get their wool cut?

A: At the BAAAbars!

3. **Q:** What happened to the cat that swallowed a ball of wool?

A: She had mittens!

4. **Q:** Why is the crab in prison?

A: Because he kept pinching things!

5. **Q:** Why shouldn't you tell a secret on a farm?

A: Because the potatoes have eyes and the corns have ears!

6. **Q:** What has four legs but cannot walk?

A: A chair!

.

7. **Q:** Why is a horse like a wedding?

A: Because they both need a groom!

8. **Q:** What is a witches' favorite subject in school?

A: Spelling!

9. **Q:** Why did the grasshopper go to the doctor?

A: Because he felt jumpy!

10. **Q.** What did the grape do when it got stepped on?

A. It let out a little wine!

11. **Q:** What did the polite ghost say to her son?

A: Don't spook until you're spoken to!

12. **Q:** What kind of roads do ghosts haunt?

A: Dead ends!

13. **Q:** Why were the early days of history called the dark ages?

A: Because there were so many knights!

14. **Q:** What kind of lighting did Noah use for the ark?

A: Floodlights!

15. **Q:** Who built the ark?

A: I have Noah idea!

16. **Q:** What did the hurricane say to the other hurricane?

A: I have my eye on you!

17. **Q:** Why couldn't the snake talk?

A: He had a frog in his throat!

.

18. **Q:** What key won't open any door?

A: A monkey!

19. **Q:** Where do chimps get their gossip?

A: On the ape vine!

20. **Q:** Why are frogs so happy?

A: Because they eat what bugs them!

21. **Q:** What did one wall say to the other wall?

A: I'll meet you at the corner.

22. **Q:** A man arrived on Friday in a small town. He stayed for two days and left on Friday. How is this possible?

A: His horse's name is Friday!

23. **Q:** What did the paper say to the pencil?

A: Write on!

24. **Q:** What goes up and down but does not move?

A: Stairs

25. **Q:** Why couldn't the pirate play cards?

A: Because he was sitting on the deck!

26. **Q:** Why can't your nose be 12 inches long?

A: Because then it would be a foot!

27. **Q:** Why was the belt arrested?

A: Because it held up some pants!

28. **Q:** Why do you go to bed every night?

A: Because the bed won't come to you!

29. **Q:** What gets wetter the more it dries?

A: A towel.

30. **Q:** Why did the robber take a bath before robbing the bank?

A: He wanted to make a clean get away!

.

Made in the USA
San Bernardino, CA
12 April 2017